CARVING ↑
LITTLE GUYS

Easy Techniques for Beginning Woodcarvers

Keith Randich

FOX CHAPEL
PUBLISHING

Acknowledgements

To Kim and the kids, Elizabeth and Anthony, who give me the ideas for many of the figures I carve. They've become my most honest critics over time. Long gone are the days of them applauding thirty minutes of carving without injury. Now I hear, "Gee, Dad, that doesn't look like anything!"

And to Rex McHail, decoy carver and teacher extraordinaire, who bordered on relentless in his drive to get me to work on this text. This project would never have been completed without his encouragement and assistance.

To learn more about the other great books from Fox Chapel Publishing, or to find a retailer near you, call toll-free 800-457-9112 or visit us at *www.FoxChapelPublishing.com*.

We are always looking for talented authors. To submit an idea, please send a brief inquiry to acquisitions@foxchapelpublishing.com.

Printed in China
Seventh printing

Table of Contents

Introduction

This text is written with the new carver, or someone looking to try carving, in mind. The instructions, with accompanying photographs, take the reader cut-by-cut from a small block of wood to a completed Little Guy. Experienced carvers should expect to move through these steps fairly quickly, adding their own ideas to the figure as they go. There seems to be no shortage of books in print showing how to carve cowboys, hillbillies, Santas, and hermits, so it is my intent to use an occupational study that most of us are more familiar with on an everyday basis: the executive. If your boss is a great person, you could carve a caricature of him. If not, I'm sure psychologists everywhere would agree about the therapeutic value of a knife in one hand and a representation of your authority figure in the other. Just be sure to keep track of your thumbs. But anyway, with a little change here or there, the executive can become a soldier, hunter, fireman, doctor, fisherman, Native American, and so on.

I'd like to add a disclaimer here before we get going. The book is about carving Little Guys, but please don't think I have anything against carving Little Gals, or Little Girls, or even Little Women. Some of my favorite carvings are females, as are my favorite wife and daughter. My intent is simply to avoid a text full of he/she, his/her, and Guy/Girl. Thanks for understanding.

Before We Get Started

Before we get into carving, here are some of the basic things you need to know.

Wood

Clockwise from bottom left: tupelo, basswood, cedar, pine, jelutong.

In general, any straight-grained, relatively soft wood can be carved into a Little Guy. I've been successful with basswood, pine, cedar, cottonwood, tupelo, catalpa, butternut, and even a piece of spruce split from last year's Christmas tree. Because the figures are so small, you can get away with carving a harder piece of wood than you may be tempted to try with a larger carving. I do urge you to try carving different kinds of wood, especially found wood. Cut the wood into 1" x 1" (25mm x 25mm) squares anywhere from 1½" to 2½" (38mm to 64mm) in length, and give it a few months to dry in the proverbial "warm and

dry" location before carving. I'm pretty impatient when it comes to waiting around for the blocks to dry, so I often use the drying kiln that my builder thoughtfully included in my basement (it doubles as the ductwork for my forced-air heating system).

For your first couple of Little Guys, I suggest using basswood cut into blocks that are 1" (25mm) square and 2" (51mm) long. Basswood is probably the most popular carving wood and should be readily available to you. Many craft stores and hardwood lumber stores carry basswood specifically for carvers.

Knives

Little Guys can be carved from start to finish with a single knife. Having proven this statement a number of times hasn't helped this affliction I have for buying every new knife that comes along, but it is true nonetheless.

When selecting a knife, look for one that was intended to be used for whittling and woodcarving. The tip of the knife should come to a point, and the length of the exposed blade shouldn't exceed 1½" (38mm). The most important criteria for a good knife is that it must be razor-sharp. Most tool companies do a fair job of sharpening their knives before shipment, but they are still relying on the purchaser to do the final honing.

There are a couple of toolmakers out there that sell knife handles, along with an assortment of replaceable blades for the handle. This concept makes an excellent knife for someone who wants to start making Little Guys. The blades are well-made and usually require a minimum amount of honing before they are put to use. They are inexpensive to buy, so if you nick the edge or just can't seem to get it razor-sharp, replace the blade.

Honing

Sharpening is when you shape the edge of a tool to fit the job you're performing. Honing is simply polishing that edge until it is extremely sharp. Sharpening can involve a variety of tools and techniques, but we'll get off fairly inexpensively with honing. All we'll need for honing is a piece of leather at least 6" (152mm) long. Old belts work great. Rub a little polishing compound on the rough side of the leather, and clamp it or glue it to a flat surface. Place the blade flat on the leather, tilt the knife slightly onto its cutting edge, and drag it across the leather surface with the cutting edge trailing. Turn the blade over and pull it back in the opposite direction.

You can easily repeat this process for five minutes or so in order to get a new knife well honed. I've heard about carvers testing the final sharpness of an edge by cutting arm hairs or shaving a curl from a thumbnail. These would be adequate tests if we intended to carve arm hairs or thumbnails, but since it's wood we want to carve, test the edge on a scrap of wood, preferably across the grain. The knife should cut cleanly through the wood. If it leaves a torn edge or is difficult to pull through the cut, keep honing. Some blades need more work than others.

Cutting

Stop cut

The intent of this cut is to define some detail in the carving. The cut is executed by pushing the edge of the blade straight into the wood. A long stop cut is made by pushing the tip of the blade edge into the wood, and then pulling the knife while keeping the tip buried in the wood.

Slicing cut

The purpose of this cut is to shave away the wood. The blade is angled slightly, and then pulled through the wood. The slicing cut often follows a stop cut. The stop cut defines a detail, and then the slicing cut removes the wood from around that detail to allow it to stand out.

Safety

You're going to be pulling and pushing a razor-sharp knife blade into a tiny block of wood that is held in your free hand.

Let's face it—the potential for an accident does exist. There are a few tips to keep them to a minimum. First of all, make your cuts small. We aren't going to remove a lot of wood, so taking deep cuts isn't going to save you much time. Whenever possible, pull the knife toward your thumb while cutting. I know this goes against your Boy Scout experience, but more control is gained.

If you must push the blade in order to make a particular cut, use the thumb of your free hand, placed on the back of the blade, to do the pushing. Protect the thumb on your knife hand with a commercially available thumb guard. A bandage on the inside of the thumb joint will work in a pinch. The best tip for carving safety is to keep your blade sharp. Most accidents occur from forcing a dull knife into the wood. If you find yourself having to apply too much pressure on a cut, stop and spend some time honing the blade.

Repairs

Occasionally the knife edge travels a little bit farther than you intended, and a piece of wood splits off your figure. The first order of business is to find that piece. If you feel that the figure needs to have it back on, white glue and a rubber band will put you back in business. Let the glue dry before resuming carving. The Santa pictured above is being reunited with his "nose like a cherry." I don't recommend using any of the "superglues" on your Little Guy to speed up the process, as they have a tendency to dull knife blades. Use a little creativity as you're facing a repair. The damage may be done, but you may have an opportunity to turn your figure into something other than originally intended. Cowboy hats can turn into baseball caps, fireman hats, or (if you're really having a tough day) stocking hats. Chubby guys can turn into skinny guys, and hands can disappear into pockets. The last thing you want to do is to toss the poor guy. Because we're working on a caricature of a person, the worst that can happen is that you end up with an ugly Little Guy.

Steps in Carving a Little Guy

1. Begin by shaping the top of your Little Guy's head. Starting about ½" (13mm) from the top, carve off the top edges of the block by using a slicing cut that ends at the very tip of the head. Continue to turn the block and slice off the ridges left by your knife cuts.

Continue slicing until the top of the head appears round. Take both a bird's-eye and profile view of the block to check your progress. The closer you get to round, the lighter your cuts become. Keep carving those corners until it appears that a ball is growing out of your block.

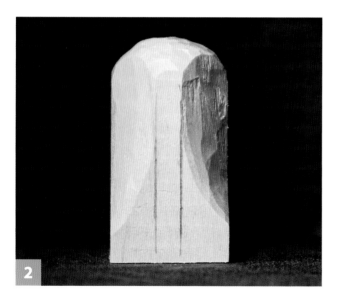

2. Successful Little Guys always seem to be those with highly exaggerated features such as noses, boots, bellies, etc. Making these features more developed is simply a matter of making them stand out on your figure. This next step will help force you to carve the nose and belly well out in front of the Little Guy by slicing away the front corners of your block from the ankles to the head.

On the front of your block, draw two parallel lines ¼" (6mm) apart from head to toe. On each side of the block, draw a single line in the middle, also from head to toe. Starting about ½" (13mm) from the bottom of your block, make an in-and-up slicing cut on the front corners and carry the cut right out through the head. Continue slicing away, using the lines drawn as your guides. When completed, the front of the figure will have a V shape.

3. Carve the sharp edges off the back of the block.

4. Our next step is to draw on the head. On a human, the head is between ½ and ⅛ of the total length of the body. At that scale our Little Guy's head would be ¼" (6mm) in length. Later on in this text, we'll spend quite a bit of time on carving the face. Quite honestly, the face will stand out more than anything else on your figure. The clothing and accessories will suggest the interest or occupation of the finished piece, but the face is what gives these carvings their character. Therefore, we're going to need some room to carve these faces and will accomplish this by making the head anywhere from ⅓ to ½ the total length of the block. On smaller blocks, you could go as far as to use ¾ of the block as a head. (This is very helpful if you find you're not adept at carving pants.)

Draw a chin line about ⅞" (22mm) down from the top of the block. At the back of the neck, draw a short line ½" (13mm) down from the top of the block. Connect these with sloping lines around the sides of the face.

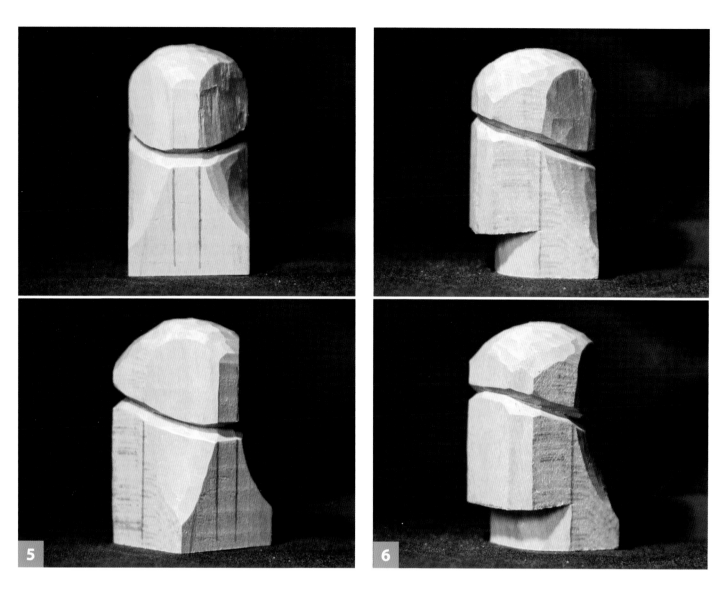

5. Separate the head from the rest of the body by making a number of small cuts around the line drawn in Step 4. Push the knife edge straight into the line to make a stop cut, and then carefully pop out small chips by slicing into the stop cut at a 45° angle from above and below. Continue making these small cuts around the neck until you've gone at least ⅛" (3mm) deep all around the figure.

6. Draw a line around the sides and back of the figure to lay out the bottom of the coat. This line is about ⅜" (10mm) from the bottom of the block and runs from the midpoint line drawn on the side of the figure in Step 2 to the midpoint line on the other side. Push the knife edge straight in on the line to make a stop cut, then make a slicing cut up from the bottom of the block to pop out a chip. Keep making these cuts until the coat stands out about ⅛" (3mm) around the sides and back.

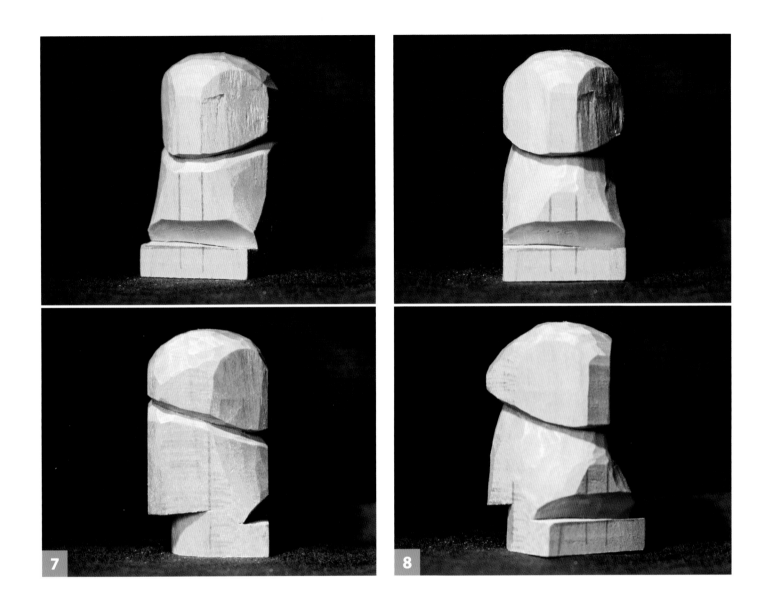

7. Draw a horizontal line ¼" (6mm) from the bottom of the block for the front of the shoes. Make a stop cut on this line, and then pop out a chip by carving down from the belly at a 45° angle. Start this belly cut about ½" (13mm) from the bottom of the block. Make the stop cut deeper and keep popping out chips until the cut is at least ¼" (6mm) deep. This cut will help to give us the highly developed belly and shoes that I talked about earlier.

8. We'll take a short break here from the major modeling cuts and spend a few minutes rounding off the figure and cleaning up the cuts made so far. We want to make sure that we're using a really sharp blade, so take time to hone your edge.

Round the edges on the front and sides of the Little Guy. Start your cuts at the belly and bring them right up into the chin and jaw. Recut the stop cuts under the chin and jaw. Don't remove too much wood from the belly at this point. Gently round over the edges from the back to the base of the neck. Round off the top and sides of the head.

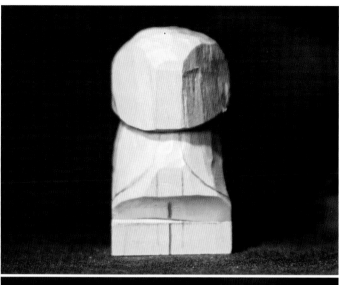

9. Now we're going to draw in some details on the figure. On the back, draw a line from the Little Guy's coat down to his feet in the center of the block to separate the legs. Draw a similar line on the front from the inseam to the shoes, and make a mark down the center of the shoes as well. On the sides of the head, draw an upside down V about ¼" (6mm) in length starting at the neckline. This line will define both the jaw and hairlines. Starting under the chin, draw in two lines that connect with the coat lines we carved in Step 6 to represent the front of the coat. Curve the lines out at the belly so they blend into the stop cut on the bottom of the coat. The last features we want to draw in are the arms. Draw the arms on the sides of the figure well back from the belly. Draw circles for the hands and place them at the same height on the Little Guy as his belly.

10. Make a deep stop cut on the line separating the back of the legs. Using just the tip of the knife blade, round off both sides of the stop cut to further separate the legs. This cut should start from the bottom of the block and carry right up to the rear end of the Little Guy. Check your progress by sighting down the underside of the block.

11. The next step is to define the shoes. Starting at the center of the shoes, make very small stop cuts at a 45° angle toward the centerline. These cuts will form a V between the shoes. Carefully continue these cuts until the V reaches back to the legs.

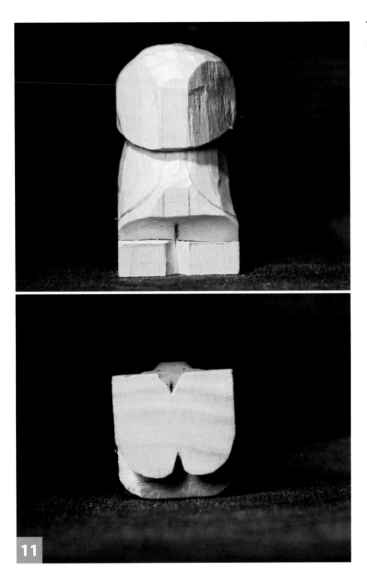

12. Separating the front of the legs is similar to the process of cutting the rear in Step 10. Start with a deep stop cut down the line from the Little Guy's inseam to his shoes. Use the tip of your blade to round over this cut on both sides as you did with the back of the legs, but this time, start the cut at the inseam and slice down to the shoes.

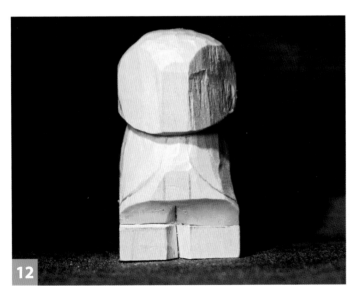

13. We're going to pop out the small V-shaped piece of wood to form the jaw/hairline on either side of the head. Use the tip of your blade to make stop cuts on both sides of the V. Make progressively deeper stop cuts until you've reached the depth of the shoulder/chest area. Starting from the chest, make a slicing cut up into the V to pop it out. Once the V is out, make tiny stop cuts to round off the edges of the jaw and hairlines.

14. Carefully outline the arms and hands with stop cuts. Progressively make these cuts deeper, but keep in mind that the cuts should be more shallow as you move toward the shoulder. The cut should be near the surface at the armpit, but almost ⅛" (3mm) deep around the hand. Starting at the bottom edge of the coat, slice up to the stop cut at the hand. Starting from the bottom edge of the coat, use the tip of the blade to slice away the wood along both sides of the arm. As you near the elbow, start to bring the knife out of the cut so the blade exits the wood at the armpit level. Continue this cut until the arm stands out from the chest and back. Use a slicing cut to round the edges left by these cuts. They should flow gently into the chest and back areas of the coat.

15. Once you have the front of the coat cleaned up, we can define its placement on the chest and belly. Because our figure has a pronounced belly, the coat has a tendency to open wider as we move down from the neck. Because we've probably carved away the lines we drew earlier for the coat, draw them back on with this opening in mind. Using just the knife tip, start at the neck and make a stop cut that curves right into the line defining the bottom of the coat. Make slicing cuts from below the coat into this stop cut until the coat stands out from the legs about ⅛" (3mm) at the bottom and, like the arm cut, gets more shallow as you move up to the neck.

16. The trick to successfully carving shoes is to avoid getting too carried away when carving the details. I try to give each figure's shoes that "clodhopper" look. The area we have left for the shoes on your figure should be about ¼" (6mm) tall and at least that wide. At this point, we want to do two things to the shoes, and both call for light, delicate cuts. The first step is to round off the inside and outside front corners. Check your progress by holding the character upside down. The second step is round off the tops of the shoes. Take very small cuts to do this. It may seem that you aren't accomplishing much, but just keep knocking off the edges. Don't go more than halfway down the side of the shoe to carve—stick to the tops of the shoes.

17. Draw the bottom of the pant legs. Start at the stop cut that separated the back of the legs, about ⅛" (3mm) from the bottom of the carving. Draw a sloping line around to the front where the fronts of the pant legs meet the tops of the shoes. Make a shallow stop cut on this line, and then carve into this cut by carefully slicing up at an angle from the shoes.

18. Now let's start some serious work on the face. We have already carved the face into a V shape, and now we'll want to continue to carve that V to more of a point at the nose. Make a small X in the center of the front of the head. The tip of the nose will be slightly below this mark. Starting at the jawline, carefully slice up the sides of the face until the point of the V on the center of the face is more pronounced.

The next step ensures that the nose becomes the most prominent part of the face. Place your blade about ⅛" (3mm) below the X, and slice back to the hairline to create the bridge of the nose. Continue making this cut until the bridge flows back from its tip to the hairline. Check your progress by viewing the profile of the head. When this step is complete, the tip of the nose will be a point near the center of the head, and the rest of the face will be sloping away from the tip in three directions.

19. Make a stop cut across the face just slightly below the tip of the nose. Slice out a chip by carving up into the stop cut from below. This cut defines the distance the nose will stick out from the face. Be careful making this cut, as the nose is delicate and will pop off if the knife blade hits it.

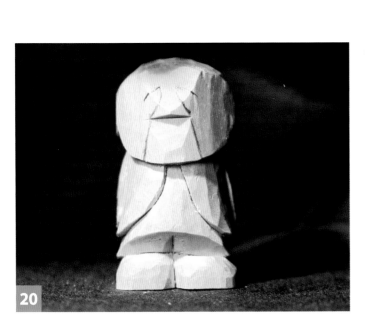

20. Draw on cheek lines that start at the outsides of the base of the nose and curve down and out away from the chin. Draw the remainder of the nose from the base to the bridge. Curve this line in as you approach the bridge. Starting at the bridge, draw two straight lines down at an angle about ¼" (6mm) long for the eyebrows.

21. Using just the tip of the blade, carve curved stop cuts about ⅛" (3mm) deep along the lines drawn during Step 20. Slice away the wood on the outside of the stop cuts that defined the nose. Use just the tip of the blade, and carry the slice right up to the brow.

Slice away the wood on the inside of the stop cut that defined the cheek line. Again, use just the tip of the blade and slice from the chin up to the nose.

22. Round off the mouth area with the tip of your knife. Round over the chin into the neck.

23. Using just the tip of your blade, round the edges of the nose and the jaw. Take tiny cuts to avoid carving the whole nose away.

24. Now, carve the hair on the Little Guy's head. Starting at the neck, make a very shallow stop cut up to the top of the head, while holding the blade on a slight angle. Recut this same line holding the blade at the opposite angle. This second cut will remove a long, slender slice of wood. Take the time to repeat these cuts until your figure has a full head of hair.

25. Draw the mouth on the face about midway between the nose and chin. Using just the tip of the blade, make a stop cut on the line. Widen this line by recutting the mouth with the blade angled slightly toward the nose.

26. Let's add a lower lip to our figure. Start by carving a little more wood away from the chin. Use an in-and-down slicing cut about 1⁄16" (2mm) below the mouth, which will leave a little mound for the lower lip. Round the chin into the neck. Slice away the edges on the jaw line, rounding these over into the neck as well.

27. Using the tip of the blade, round over the hands and arms. Draw three lines on each hand to define the fingers. Make stop cuts on each line. Widen these lines by carefully recutting each stop cut, angling the blade in either direction to round over the fingers. Use the tip of the blade to round the fingers until they appear similar in width.

Cut a shallow V across the wrist to separate the hand from the arm. Blend this cut into the hand and the arm.

28. Draw a line on each shoe about 1⁄16" (2mm) from the bottom for the soles. Cut a shallow stop cut on the line. Widen the stop cut by recutting it with the blade angled slightly toward the top of the figure.

29

29. Your Little Guy is pretty well finished. The only thing we have left to do is to draw on the clothing and make light stop cuts to carve them in. I want to stop you at this point to urge you to add another step to the process.

You've put a few hours in on this carving, and when you get this close to being done, there is a real temptation to carve on the clothes and begin painting. However, this is the last chance we'll have to go back and clean up the cuts on this figure. Take the time to hone the blade of your knife and clean up the cuts on your Little Guy one more time. Round over corners, and recut the bottoms of stop cuts and V-cuts. Look for balance and symmetry in the face, shoulders, arms, legs, and coat. Make sure your blade is sharp, and take very light cuts. Other carvers will notice your attention to this detail right away, and it shows that you have a little pride in the work you do.

The clothing of your Little Guy is limited only by your own creativity. At the very least, you'll want a couple of parallel lines across the belly for a pant and belt line. You can add a couple of vertical lines from the belt to the neck for a shirt. Other possibilities include buttons, pockets, a shirt collar, coat lapels, a necktie, etc. Cut these lines with very shallow stop cuts. Widen these lines by recutting them with the blade angled slightly. Make sure that the bottoms of the stop cuts are clean. Your carving will look more skillfully executed, and it will make the painting much easier.

Finishing

You can go in a number of different directions to finish your Little Guys. Many carvers like the look of the wood and simply dip their figures in an oil finish and buff until dry. Spraying on several light coats of polyurethane, taking time to let each coat dry, would do a nice job as well.

Painting the Little Guys is an opportunity to really bring them alive. I've had quite a bit of luck with both watercolors and acrylics, but don't use them straight from the tube or jar. Mix water with your paint at about five parts to one. This turns the paint into more of a stain. I brush on the mixture, and then blot it out with a small rag. Take a clean rag and rub off as much of the stain as you can. This will leave dark shades in the low spots and light shades on the high spots. In addition, the rubbing burnishes the wood slightly, leaving a glow on the surface.

You can paint your figures using just a #2 and a #000 brush. Apply your lightest colors first (white, yellow, flesh), and gradually moving to the dark ones. Rubbing the darker colors will mess up those light colors applied earlier. After the figures are completely painted, go back and redo the lightest colors again.

For the eyes, paint a circle (or oval) of white about ⅛" (3mm) in diameter in each eye channel. Allow it to dry. Next, take the color you are using for the irises and place a medium circle of it in the

middle of the white. Place the irises off-center to make your Little Guy look off to the side, up, or down. The last step is to add a white gleam to the eye. Don't overdo this. A gleam is a dot the size of a pencil tip that makes the eye come alive. Place it right in the center of the iris.

Let your carving dry overnight. To help protect it, give it a light dusting of clear polyurethane. Write the wood type, date, and your signature on the bottom to complete the figure.

Adding On to the Basic Little Guy

Making a few changes to the Little Guy just completed can turn your executive into a new figure with a different occupation and personality type. The following are some examples of additions and changes to make to your next carving.

Faces

You could carve dozens of executives, paint them all in identical colors, and never have two look the same simply by altering the face. Add a moustache under the nose between the two cheek lines. Angle the cheek lines to different degrees. Be sure to widen the lines to give yourself more mouth area to work with. Instead of carving a simple mouth line, carve an open smile and add teeth. Drill a tiny hole in one end of the mouth, and stick in a little cigar. Drop the chin line lower when first laying out the head shape and add a beard. Alter the nose shape. Make the biggest nose you can possibly fit on the face.

Practice making faces on a separate block of wood. Use just the corners of the block and carve nothing but faces, one on top of another, in a sort of totem pole fashion. Experiment with different mouth shapes. Notice that a simple little turn of the knife point here or there can completely change the expression on your Little Guy's face.

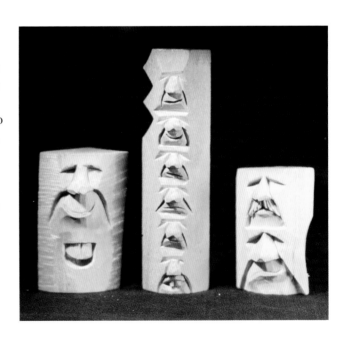

Ears

Adding ears to your figure should take place early in the head-shaping process. I usually leave out the V that we carved to separate the jaw/hairline (Step 13) and place the ears in that location instead.

Draw ¼" (6mm) circles on the sides of the head. Make a stop cut using just the tip of the blade about ⅛" (3mm) deep. Carefully slice away the wood around the ear and blend it in with the rest of the head. The ear should clearly stand out from the rest of the head. Push the tip of the blade into the center of the ear and slowly twist the blade completely around to dig out the inside of the ear. Use the tip of the knife to clean up the inside of the ear.

Hats

Little Guys love wearing hats. Hats help define who the figure is supposed to be. A hat is the first thing you carve on a Little Guy when starting with a new block. Make an in-and-up cut on the top ½" (13mm) of the block to cut in the crown of the hat. Keep turning the block and making this cut until the crown is set in at least ¼" (6mm) all the way around. Round off the top of the crown. So far, you have completed the crown of the hat, as well as the top of the brim. Use a pencil to lay out the bottom of the brim by drawing a line ⅛" (3mm) below the top of the brim. Push your knife edge straight in right below this line, and then pop out a tiny chip by slicing up from below at a 45° angle into this stop cut. Continue these cuts all the way around the figure until the cut is ⅛" (3mm) deep. Don't make this cut too deep, or the hat will appear to be a couple of sizes too small. Also, keep in mind that the hat brim is very delicate and care must be taken when carving around it.

This basic hat design can be altered to create a number of styles. Carve away all but the front brim for a baseball cap or all but the rear for a fireman's hat. Flatten the crown for a cowboy hat, or make the crown extra long for a ten-gallon number.

Hands

The hands are used to hold the belongings of your Little Guy. Many of the accessories I make for the figures start out as toothpicks: a pool cue, cane, fishing pole, golf club, etc. Drill a ¹⁄₁₆" (2mm) hole through the side of the hand to hold the toothpicks in place. The position of the hand needs to be determined when you draw the arm on the block in Step 9.

Hands that are holding a purse can hang straight down. Hands holding a pool cue need to have their arms bent at a right angle at the elbow, and then extended across the front of the figure. The hand would be in the middle of the belly, with the thumb pointing up.

You can give your Little Guy a casual look by placing his hands in his pockets. Draw the arms bent at the elbow and coming down toward the front of the body at a 45° angle. Let the arms stand out from the body about ⅛" (3mm) at the elbow, but make sure this cut tapers out as you move to the wrist to give the appearance of the arm entering the body at the pocket. Start this slicing cut at the wrist, and make it gradually deeper as you move to the elbow. Start a second cut at the shoulder and make it gradually deeper as it moves to the elbow. Cut a shallow stop cut at the wrist for a pocket.

Feet

The basic footwear for Little Guys is the chunky shoe. Add vertical cuts every ¹⁄₁₆" (2mm) around the soles, paint them white, and you've got your first pair of gym shoes for more athletically inclined Little Guys. Small, flat pieces could be attached to the bottoms of the shoes to turn them into skis. Four tiny pieces of a ⅛" (3mm) dowel on the bottom of each shoe puts your figure into roller skates.

To make the shoes into feet, make lines about ⅛" (3mm) long on top of the feet to separate the toes. Leave plenty of room for a big toe. Your critics will never notice that you made only four toes, but they will notice if all the toes are identical in size. Make very small stop cuts on these lines. Deepen these lines by recutting them at a slight angle. Take these lines down the front of the foot to the bottom of the block. Do not go very deep at all in the front, as you can easily break off a piece of the foot. Carefully round off the tops of the toes.

Other Tools

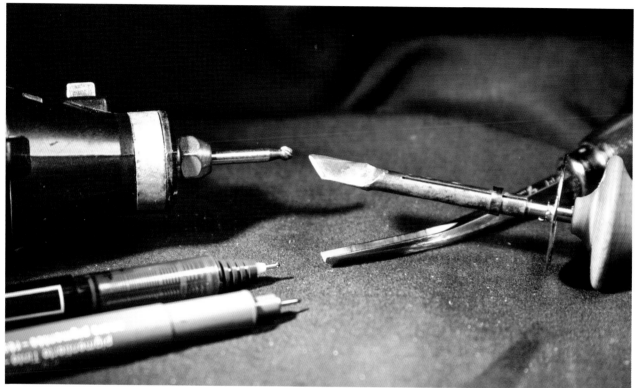

Clockwise from bottom left: technical pens, motorized grinder with ball cutter, woodburner, V-tool (red handle).

I put this text together with the goal of having a beginning carver create his first couple of Little Guys with a single tool. Once you get rolling, there are other tools that come in handy to make some of the cuts described earlier, as well as some operations that require a specialty tool.

A tiny V-tool is great for shaping the sides of the nose, putting in hair, and outlining the clothes. A ¼" (6mm) gouge in the shape of a half-circle makes very quick work of defining the ears. Just push it straight in, pull out, roll to the other side, push in again, and the ear is laid out in a perfect circle.

A small woodburner is a lot of fun to use on these figures. You can put hair, eyebrows, moustaches, and beards on your figures easily. Don't think you have to go out and buy a professional model, either. I've had success using one from an inexpensive woodburning kit that many craft stores carry.

If the woodburner doesn't appeal to you, and you still want to add tiny details to the finished carving, try a technical pen. Many office supply stores sell inexpensive pens in the .2mm to .1mm range. Buy a dark color for putting in eyebrows, moustaches, and (my favorite) a tattoo.

Finally, a small, motorized grinder equipped with a ⅛" (3mm) ball cutter does a nice job of cleaning the inside of ears and also works great as a drill.

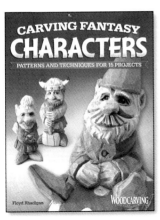

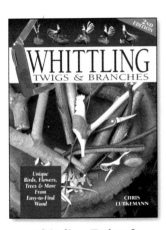